Faithful

LIVING

HONORING GOD THROUGH PERSISTENCE
AND FAITH DURING TRYING TIMES

DONALD R. RUTH

ISBN 978-1-63903-997-5 (paperback)
ISBN 978-1-63903-998-2 (digital)

Christian Faith Publishing, Inc.
832 Park Avenue
Meadville, PA 16335
www.christianfaithpublishing.com

Printed in the United States of America

I dedicate this book to my parents, George and Susie Ruth. Though both are now with the Lord, together they instilled in me the values that I now possess. I thank God for the love they gave to me and to each of my siblings. Though I miss them greatly, it is my hope that through this book, I am able to pass on some of the things they imparted unto me. Love forever!

I also dedicate this book to my wife, Bernice, who has always been my inspiration. I love you and always will. Thank you for always being there, providing me with the encouragement, discernment, and support that I so often need.

I further dedicate this book to my daughters, Antigone and Fatemah. You have made me so proud. Both of you love God, and both of you are successful in your chosen professions. I could not ask for a better set of girls than you. I love you with all my heart.

Moreover, I dedicate this book to my son-in-law Eric, whom I view as my son. Your love for God is unquestionable, and you are truly a gifted man of God; one who is a godly leader for your wife, Fatemah, and for your son, Elijah.

Lastly, I dedicate this book to my awesome grandsons, Royce and Elijah. You are my heartbeats, and Pawpaw just cannot get enough of you. As you grow older, just know that God has great things in store for you. Stay close to Him, and He will bring those things to pass.

Contents

Acknowledgments

I wish to acknowledge the congregation of St. John Baptist Church of Alsen, the church where I was baptized and where I received my primary Christian education. Thank you for allowing me to serve you as pastor for the last twenty-four and a half years. Your support of the vision that God gave me for St. John has been steady throughout the years, and I trust that I have served you well. It is my heart's desire that I continue to serve you in a way that pleases God and blesses you.

I was particularly blessed to see how we were able to navigate through the COVID-19 crisis of 2020 and 2021. How, during this pandemic, new ministries were birthed forth and existing ministries met the challenge with innovation and adaptability.

As I said to you many times before, "There is no church like St. John."

I love you all!

Introduction

It is my prayer that this book becomes a source of strength to you in your everyday life. As a point of guidance, unless otherwise noted, all scriptural references used will be from the *King James Version* translation.

Scripture remains strong, convicting, convincing, and relevant in today's world, despite the many attempts underway to nullify its potency. With this in mind, in writing this book, I lean heavily on scripture to substantiate much of my comments. I was particularly drawn to the words of the Apostle Paul in his letter to the church at Corinth, recorded in 1 Corinthians 4:1–2, "Let a man so account of us, as of the ministers of Christ and stewards of the mysteries of God. Moreover it is required in stewards, that a man be found faithful."

Though the apostle was writing specifically from the perspective of apostolic leadership, his message is nonetheless applicable to all believers, regardless of ministerial status or position. Paul, the anointed man of God, is reminding believers today that there are onlookers, those who see us in our daily lives. These onlookers see both our witness and our walk as believers. Thus, they have a right to hold us accountable as ministers of Christ.

The word *minister* is properly translated as *servant*. Believers are servants of Christ, and within our duties as Christ's servants, we are stewards of the mysteries of God. A *steward* is one who manages the affairs, the property, or the business of another. The Greek word for steward in the abovementioned text is *oi-ko-no-mos* which means overseer. Believers are, therefore, overseers of the mysteries of God. In other words, God has entrusted believers with the mysteries of Himself.

The obvious question is, what are the *mysteries of God*, and what do they entail? Mysteries in the New Testament are things that had, at one time, been hidden, but now revealed to God's people (gotquestions.org). They are things that cannot be understood or comprehended by the natural man. Only through the aid of the Holy Spirit can man truly come to understand and comprehend the mysteries of God. The mystery that Paul is referring to in this context is the Gospel, the Word of God. God has entrusted believers to steward or oversee it, the Gospel, in the earth realm.

In stewarding the Gospel, one must share it willingly, readily, and accurately. However, proper stewardship of the Gospel involves more than just the preaching and teaching of it. The Gospel must also be lived. Notwithstanding the power of preaching and teaching, there are those who will be moved toward Christ by the ways and lifestyles of believers that they witness.

Believers, who are stewards of the Gospel, whether their stewardship be through preaching, teaching, or living, are required to be faithful. Paul's words here make no mention of the need for eloquence, giftedness, or talent, only faithfulness. And that amounts to faithfulness in living.

Faithful living is living in obedience to the will of God. Despite trials, despite circumstances, and despite obstacles, it means remaining committed to God in all things. In this season, God is looking for faithfulness, and there is a blessing and benefit attached to being faithful.

Hebrews 3:14 (NLT) states, "For if we are faithful to the end, trusting God just as firmly as when we first believed, we will share in all that belongs to Christ."

God will always reward faithfulness, and I repeat, in this season, God is looking for faithfulness. Faithfulness boils down to persistency, that is, staying the course laid out by God.

In this book, I want to discuss a few areas where God expects faithfulness or persistence on the part of His servants. The areas that I will discuss are primary and are not all inclusive. But it is my belief that if we stay true in these areas, then on that day when we stand before Christ, we will hear Him pronounce to us the words found in Matthew 25:21, "Well done, thou good and faithful servant: thou hast been faithful over a few things, I will make thee ruler over many things: enter thou into the joy of thy lord."

Chapter 1

PERSISTENCE IN PROBLEMS

Having predestinated us unto the adoption of children by Jesus
Christ to himself, according to the good pleasure of his will.

—Ephesians 1:5

But when the fulness of the time was come, God sent forth his
Son, made of a woman, made under the law, to, redeem them
that were under the law, that we might receive the adoption
of sons. And because ye are sons, God hath sent forth the
Spirit of his Son into your hearts, crying, Abba, Father.

—Galatians 4:4–6

From the above scriptures, we can conclude that believers have a
heavenly parent in the person of God. And as any good parent,
God is concerned about the health and well-being of us, His children. Out of His concern for us, He makes decisions concerning our
lives that are intended to lead us to the path of a balanced Christian

life. A balanced Christian life is a life of routine faithfulness. Routine faithfulness is everyday faithfulness.

In life, most of our experiences tend to be more commonplace as compared to experiences that are either mountaintop or valley low in nature. Most people can usually gird themselves for the unusual; they can get prepared for the difficult, they can get up for the big game, if you will. However, our main struggle is with the routine, the mundane, the commonplace challenges in life. Song of Solomon 2:15 states, "It is the little foxes that spoil the vines." God wants us to be faithful in all things, not just the big things. And this is where God judges our faithfulness, in the routine things of life.

There are many different areas of faithfulness. But there is one area of faithfulness that God watches closely. It is faithfulness in problems. Some people are faithful until problems show up, then their faithfulness abandons them. But I want you to know that God wants us to be faithful, especially when problems arise.

In every problem that we face, understand that God could have stopped it from ever becoming a problem. If He chose not to stop it, then He is expecting us to endure and be a living witness for Him in the process. Consider this hypothetical situation.

You are active in your church and community. You are trying to live right. You are trusting God and trying to do what is right. You are trying to set a good example for your children, and yet, you are having all these problems—struggling to make your ends meet, your children are not doing what they should be doing, or perhaps sickness has invaded in your body. All these problems have come your way, and you are doing your best to honor God with your life.

Then you look across the street and see your neighbor who does not confess Christ, who does not associate with any church, who lives a life of revelry, and who has issues with these so-called Christians. Yet his children are getting scholarships to go to college; the entire household drives nice vehicles while the car that you are driving is on its last leg. It appears that this neighbor, who does not even try to honor God, has no problems whatsoever while you, the one who is trying to honor God, appears to have all the problems. And as you continue to ponder on this situation, you begin developing what I call a Job complex. Allow me to explain what a Job complex is.

A quick review of Job's story is necessary. Job was indeed a true man of God. The Bible describes him as being blameless and upright. He was also a very wealthy man, so much so that he was viewed as "the greatest of all the men in the east" (Job 1:3). He was a man who feared God and shunned evil (Job 1:1). Yet God permitted and allowed Satan to attack Job, and Satan, in doing so, held no punches. On a certain day, Job experienced a series of life-altering tragedies all orchestrated by Satan.

First, a raiding party of the Sabeans came and took Job's oxen and his donkeys and slaughtered Job's servants who were attending them. Next, a fire fell from heaven and burned up all of Job's sheep and the servants who were attending them. Thirdly, a raiding party of the Chaldeans came and took all of Job's camels and killed the servants who attended them. Job had ten children, and they all were killed on that same day by a storm that caused the house where they were gathered to collapse upon them. Again, these tragic events all happened on the same day. Job's reaction to these series of tragedies is recorded in Job 1:20–22:

> Then Job arose, and rent his mantle, and shaved his head, and fell down upon the ground, and worshipped, And said, Naked came I out of my mother's womb, and naked shall I return thither: the Lord gave, and the Lord hath taken away; blessed be the name of the Lord. In all this Job sinned not, nor charged God foolishly.

Through this obviously painful and heart-wrenching day and period in Job's life, he nevertheless remained faithfully persistent in his problem. However, Satan asked God for permission to attack Job a second time, and God again permitted him to do so. Only this time, Satan attacked Job's health. He smote Job with painful boils all over his body. As Job dealt with this issue, his wife confronted him, demanding that he curse God and die (Job 2:9). Apparently, she had given up on God and had developed a disdain for Job and his faith in God, who had allowed all these tragedies to happen. Job rebuffed his wife, and the Bible records that in all this, Job did not sin with his lips (Job 2:10).

However, as time progressed, Job began to develop some doubt within. His doubt was concerning the fairness of God, and he speaks his heart in Job 12:6, "The tabernacles of robbers prosper, and they that provoke God are secure; into whose hand God bringeth abundantly."

Job was saying that it looks like God is blessing those who do not honor Him, and by default, He does not appear to be concerned about those who do. This is what I call a Job complex. A Job complex is a false perception of God that is birthed out of a state of continual pain in which there appears to be no relief. However, such a mindset within believers is the result of a failure to remember one thing. And the one thing they fail to remember is something that I said earlier, "We have a heavenly parent in the person of God." And God will take care of His children.

Knowing this, we must never compare ourselves to others who have not been born again or to someone who is not trying to honor God with his or her life. While we should never elevate ourselves above others, we must also never evaluate ourselves against others. Because if they are unsaved, they do not have the same Father as you. Thus, they are not on the same path as you. God makes decisions in His children's lives that are intended always to lead to His glory and further their faithfulness.

The issues that we find ourselves facing are selected by God in order to make us better for His service. God wants us to remain faithful in our struggles as a testimony of our love for Him. Not having problems is not an indication of salvation. The fact of the matter is, one who is not saved has a major problem; they just do not realize it. God wants to get involved with our problems to show forth His glory. David said in Psalm 34:19, "Many are the afflictions of the righteous: but the LORD delivereth him out of them all."

If we are not experiencing a problem, then there is no need for deliverance. If there is no need for deliverance, then there is no need for Christ, the deliverer, to come. But if we are experiencing a problem, regardless of how big or how small it may be, then there is a need for Jesus, the deliverer, to come. And the signal for Him to come is our faithfulness or our persistence in the midst of our problem. Two verses of scripture speak to this point:

> God will repay each person according to what they have done. To those who by persistence in doing good seek glory, honor and immortality, he will give eternal life. (Romans 2:6–7 NIV)

> So let's not allow ourselves to get fatigued doing good. At the right time we will harvest a good crop if we don't give up or quit. (Galatians 6:9 MSG)

Believers must use the quickening power of the Word of God and the strengthening power of the Holy Spirit to motivate themselves during times of trouble and develop an attitude that says, "In this situation, I will not faint! In this problem, I will not give up! In this struggle, I will not quit!" Why? "Because God is expecting me to come out on the other side."

Therefore, in our problems, we must keep trusting God, we must keep doing what is right, we must keep believing, we must keep being faithful, and we must keep praising because our faithfulness is a signal flare for the Lord to come to our rescue. Consider the words of Peter:

> But may the God of all grace, who called us to His eternal glory by Christ Jesus, after you have suffered a while, perfect, establish, strengthen, and settle you. (1 Peter 5:10)

> But God shows undeserved kindness to everyone. That's why he appointed Christ Jesus to choose you to share in his eternal glory. You will suffer

for a while, but God will make you complete, steady, strong, and firm. (1 Peter 5:10 CEV)

On a personal note, both my parents were good Christian people. My father was a task-oriented, no-nonsense kind of a man, who worked hard to provide for his family. My mother had a very gentle nature and was extremely kind. She possessed a sweet spirit within. Together, they bore and raised nine children. We lived in a small house at the end of a dead-end street, and we never had much in the way material of things. I still remember some of the hard times we faced when I was a child. One particular event that happened when I was about six or seven years old remains vivid in my memory today, and it is a sample of the hard times that we faced as a family.

On a certain day, two huge men came to our house and repossessed the refrigerator because my parents had fallen behind on the payments. I happened to be inside the house when they came. I remember how my mother just stood in the corner and cried and how my father watched the men remove the appliance from the house, load it onto a truck, and then drive away. I can still see his facial expressions. They were a mixture of anger, sadness, and embarrassment.

At such a young age, I did not fully understand what was happening. However, I remember asking my mother, "How are we going to keep our food?" She replied to me, "The Lord will make a way."

My father then went outside and sidled toward the rear on the house. There, I saw him bow his head and begin to pray. Though I do not remember how everything related to the repossession turned out, and obviously, the problems that they were facing were much greater than a repossessed refrigerator. However, I do know that somehow, we made it through. My parents trusted God through this ordeal and many others. Their display of persistence in their problems helped to instill in me that same spirit of persistence. And overall, God, our heavenly parent, wants us, His children, to be persistent in our problems, knowing that He is always with us and that if we remain persistent, He will cause us to triumph.

Second Corinthians 2:14 states, "Now thanks be unto God, which always causeth us to triumph in Christ, and maketh manifest the savour of his knowledge by us in every place."

Questions to ponder

1. How can I become more persistent in problems?
2. How can I enhance my trust in God to work things out in my favor?
3. How can I motivate myself to keep fighting the good fight in the face of my struggles?

Chapter 2

PERSISTENCE IN PRAYER

And he spake a parable unto them to this end, that
men ought always to pray, and not to faint.

—Luke 18:1

Pray without ceasing.

—1 Thessalonians 5:17

Most of us pray effectually during times of crises while at all
other times we pray ritualistically, that is, we pray as part of
our spiritual regimen. Yet there is something to be said for praying
routinely. Understand that prayer is not just words uttered to God.
In his poem titled, "What is Prayer," the poet James Montgomery
writes:

> Prayer is the soul's sincere desire, Uttered or
> unexpressed,

The motion of a hidden fire, That trembles within one's beast.

Prayer is the burden of a sigh, the falling of a tear, The upward glancing of an eye, when none but God is near.

Prayer is the simplest form of speech, That infant lips can try;
Prayer, the sublimest strains that reach The Majesty on high.

Prayer is the Christian's vital breath, The Christian's native air;
His watchword at the gates of death—He enters heaven with prayer.

Prayer is the contrite sinner's voice, Returning from his ways;
While angels in their songs rejoice And cry, Behold, he prays!

Prayer is our connection to God—a connection that gives us strength and power to do the things we must do to glorify God here on earth. I want to share three perspectives about prayer that focuses on how we should pray in order to remain faithful or persistent in prayer.

First, we must pray persistently

Luke 18:1–8 contains a parable that is known to us as the parable of the unjust judge:

And he spake a parable unto them to this end, that men ought always to pray, and not to faint; Saying, There was in a city a judge, which feared

not God, neither regarded man: And there was a
widow in that city; and she came unto him, saying, Avenge me of mine adversary. And he would
not for a while: but afterward he said within himself, Though I fear not God, nor regard man; Yet
because this widow troubleth me, I will avenge
her, lest by her continual coming she weary me.
And the Lord said, Hear what the unjust judge
saith. And shall not God avenge his own elect,
which cry day and night unto him, though he
bear long with them?
I tell you that he will avenge them speedily.
Nevertheless, when the Son of man cometh, shall
he find faith on the earth?

These verses teach the importance of praying persistently. This
unnamed woman in this parable was a widow. It is important to
understand the context here, in light of the social and cultural norms
of that day. Though the rights of widows were protected under Old
Testament law, widows often found themselves under oppression and
duress at the hands of opportunistic people in society. The fact that
widows had no husbands left them exposed in a society that was
highly patriarchal.

The unnamed widow, in this parable, had apparently been
wronged by someone, who is also unnamed. In following the legal
recourse of that day, she took her issue to the court. She asked the
judge to right the wrong that had been done to her. The judge who
heard her case is given the moniker The unjust judge because he did
not fear God, nor did he respect the people whom he served. In other
words, he was void of any moral conviction, which comes from God,
and he was also lacking in empathy and compassion, which should
flow unto people as he discharged his duties.

As the judge heard the woman's case, he was unmoved and
refused her request. The scripture indicates that he maintained this
position *for a while*, which implies that he refused to move on the
woman's behalf repeatedly. This suggests that the woman kept com-

ing to him, with the same request. She was persistent! Her persistence finally paid off, as we can see in verses 4 and 5, "And he would not for a while: but afterward he said within himself, Though I fear not God, nor regard man; Yet because this widow troubleth me, I will avenge her, lest by her continual coming she weary me."

This woman kept coming to the judge, pleading her case before him, and because of her persistence, the unjust judge changed his mind and did what the woman asked of him.

If an unjust judge acts in this way to fix what is broken, to vindicate someone who has been wronged, and to restore joy to someone who was about to give up, then how much more hope should we, God's children, have in our own righteous judge, who is God Himself? The issue here is not God's faithfulness. It is whether believers like you and me will be persistent in crying out to God to fix what is broken, to vindicate those who have been wronged, and to restore the joy that Satan and life's circumstances has stolen from so many. The question is, "Will you be persistent in your praying?" Thus, Jesus says, "Men ought always to pray, and not to faint."

The Living Bible records verses 7 and 8 as follows, "Don't you think that God will surely give justice to His people who plead with Him day and night? Yes! He will answer them quickly! But the question is: When I, the Messiah, return, how many will I find who have faith and are praying?"

Think about that for a moment. When the Messiah returns, how many will He find who have faith and are praying? That is, persistently praying. Be persistent in your prayer. Don't stop praying until God gives you a release in your spirit to do so.

Secondly, we must pray intentionally

Intentional praying is praying in such a way to capitalize on key thoughts and key moments in everyday life. It is praying on purpose and praying with priority. Intentional praying requires a heart that is wide open to God and a spirit that is that is honest with self. I want to discuss two aspects of praying intentionally.

Aspect 1: Aim your prayer at your problem. In other words, don't *pray around* your problem. Whenever you can, pray specifically to your problem. This is called being intentional in your praying. While on the cross, Jesus prayed intentionally. Jesus spoke seven last words or sayings from the cross, and three of those seven last words (sayings) were in the form of intentional prayers, that is, prayers that were aimed at the problem He was facing.

Jesus's first word from the cross: "Father forgive them for they know not what they do" (Luke 23:34).

This first word dealt with the problem of ignorance on the part of those who were instrumental in crucifying the Son of God. In life, we will encounter people who may not have our best interest at heart. As a result, they may treat us wrongly, they may speak ill of us, or they may even exact out their disdain or dislike for us through some other method. Whether their actions toward us be through ignorance or otherwise, the example set forth by Jesus, as we face these situations, is to forgive. It is impossible for anyone to live a faithful life while at the same time, carry unforgiveness in their heart.

Unfortunately, unforgiveness is a sin that resides in the hearts of many. Even for those of us who love God, we often struggle with the sin of unforgiveness. If unforgiveness is not addressed, it will prevent our prayers from being heard by God. The Word of God is crystal clear on this matter, "If I regard iniquity in my heart, the Lord will not hear me" (Psalm 66:18).

Jesus prayed intentionally, asking God to forgive those who were in agreement with His crucifixion.

Jesus's fourth word from the cross: "My God, my God, why hast thou forsaken me?" (Matthew 27:46).

The fourth word dealt with the problem of feeling separated from God's love. Sin separates us from God in fellowship. Though Jesus committed no sin, He was made to be sin so that we could be made the children of righteousness in Him. Second Corinthians 5:21 states, "For He hath made Him to be sin for us, who knew not sin; that might be made the righteousness of God in him."

Prior to Jesus uttering the words found in Matthew 27:46, there was a period of darkness that lasted for three hours. It was during this period of darkness that God was transferring the sins of man onto the Savior, Jesus. Through Jesus's sacrificial death, He would pay the price for man's sin, thereby allowing sinful man to be put into a position whereby he could become reconciled to God. The darkness represents the darkness associated with sin. At the end of the period of darkness, Jesus cried out these words. Being laden with the sins of the world, Jesus, in His humanity, now felt a separation from God the Father, a separation that comes as a result of sin. Thus, He cried out to God these words.

In life, we all experience failures. Failures sometimes result from a lack of judgment, sometimes from fear, and sometimes by allowing the flesh to win. These failures can cause us to feel separated from God, who we know expects and demands better of us. Jesus identifies with this feeling, and in His experience, He cried out to God to help. He did not try to hide his feelings from God the Father; rather, He laid His feelings out before God. The point here for us is that we need to be open and honest with God as we pray. Let God know what is on your heart and cry out to Him for help.

Jesus's seventh and final word from the cross: "Father into thine hand I commend my Spirit" (Luke 23:46).

The seventh and final word dealt with the problem of releasing all to God. Jesus released His Spirit unto God, and then He died. The Greek word from which the word *commend* is interpreted means to place with someone, to commit, or to deposit. It means to release into the care of another. Jesus prayed to God the Father saying, "I am releasing my Spirit into your hands." In the same way, believers must learn how to release all into God's hand. The safety and security that we all desire is found in God's hand. The strength and blessing that we all need is found in God's hand. The task for the believer is to release unto God, and the task for God is to maintain what has been released to Him. And we know that God never fails in His duties.

Each of us knows what we need God to do in our lives. Therefore, we should aim our prayers toward the things that we need Him to do in that moment. When we pray, we must be open, we must be honest, and we must be real with God because He already knows the details anyway. He just wants us to release our issues to Him in faith. So *aim your prayer at your problem.*

Aspect 2: Align your prayers with the Word. Pray the Word. Praying the Word means praying God's Word back to Him, not to remind God of what He has said, but as an act of faith on our part, demonstrating our trust in Him and His Word. We should never ask God to do something that is contrary to His Word. I am reminded of an incident that happened many years ago at our church.

A young man came up for prayer at the end of Sunday service. When asked the nature of his prayer need, he responded by saying, "I want the church to pray for me that I get a divorce from my wife." Obviously, praying such a prayer would be in direct conflict with the Word of God. Needless to say, his prayer request was not carried out, and this person was properly counseled. But I wonder how many believers, who in their desperation, ask God to do something that is contrary to His Word?

I have found it very rewarding to quote God's Word back to Him when I pray. Recently, I experienced something that brought my spirit very low. I found myself in a state of sadness and heaviness. As I prayed to God, I said these words, "Lord, You said in Your Word that You will never leave me nor forsake me. Lord, I am in a condition where my heart is very heavy. But I'm trusting You, Lord, to help me through it and to lift up my spirit."

And God did just that. We must pray such a prayer in faith and in patience. Faith says, "I am trusting God to move in my situation," and patience says, "I am waiting on the manifestation from God."

Thirdly, we must pray fervently

James 5:16b states, "The effectual fervent prayer of a righteous man availeth much."

Effectuality speaks toward the effectiveness of the prayer, and fervency speaks toward the mannerism of the prayer. Fervent means wholehearted; it means passionate; it means powerful. So this verse is saying that a prayer that is passionate, wholehearted, and powerful will accomplish much. Thus, it is implying that a prayer that is not passionate, one that is half-hearted, one that does not have Holy Ghost power in it, will not be as effective.

Now I am not here to judge people's prayers or to critique them. But I will say this—when we pray to God, we are talking to God, the Most High King. There is an honor and a privilege in God allowing us to come before His throne in glory by prayer. So our prayers should be passionate, that is, from our spirit. They should be wholehearted, which means they should be from our heart. They should be powerful or fueled by the Holy Spirit. And when we pray prayers that are this way, things begin to happen.

I want to share another memory from my childhood. I am the sixth of nine children. The house we lived in was very small indeed, and because of its limited size and space, as a young child, I did not have a bedroom. My bed was the sofa, which happened to be in the same room as the television. To our household, this room was the living room, but to me, it was my bedroom. No matter how early I "went to bed," I really could not go to sleep until the television was turned off. Being the sixth of nine children, I did not have much sway or clout with my five older siblings. So, as you can imagine, they always won the television battle.

The good news was that, in those days, there was no cable TV or Internet, so television stations then were much fewer in number as compared to what we now have, thanks to cable TV and the Internet. Television broadcasts in our area then were limited to only two stations, and each of them ended their broadcasts at midnight. I remember that at midnight, the stations would display the American flag while playing the national anthem. When the anthem ended, so did the broadcast. The television screen would go white, and the audio would become static. Then the television would be turned off by one of my older siblings. Only then could I really go to sleep. I am not complaining about this because I enjoyed the experience of staying up late, and I really enjoyed the company of my siblings in the room. I am only setting the stage for what I'm about to say.

I cannot count the times when, during the early morning hours as I slept, I would be awakened by the sound of a person's voice. The voice that I heard would be that of my father, who would have made his way to the kitchen, which was off from the living room, my bedroom.

He would often go there to pray in the early morning hours. I believe that he would intend to pray softly, so as not to disturb me as I slept. However, as he prayed, his voice intonation would change, and his volume would increase. Though his voice never became loud, I could hear it clearly. And as he prayed, I could sense and feel the passion and the fervency with which he cried out to God.

I would hear him say such things as, "Lord, have mercy on me," "Dear Lord, bless my family and take care of my children," and "Lord Jesus, make a way for us, we need Your help." And this moved me greatly, even as a child. I never heard my father pray publicly in church or before us as a family. But I believe that God positioned me there, on that old sofa, in that living room, so that I could experience my father praying fervently for the things that he was believing God for. And God did have mercy upon him and us. God did bless us, and He did take care of us. God did step in to help us. Again, as stated in James 5:16, "The effectual fervent prayer of a righteous man availeth much."

Questions to ponder

1. How can I become more persistent in prayer?
2. What are some of my real prayer needs today?
3. How can I pray and learn to wait on God?

Chapter 3

PERSISTENCE IN PRAISE

In chapter 1, I discussed persistence in problems. I said that in our problems, we must keep trusting God, we must keep believing God, and we must keep on doing what is right because our faithfulness becomes a signal flare for the Lord to come to our rescue. In chapter 2, I discussed persistence in prayer. How we must remain faithfully persistent in our prayer lives. I said that we must pray persistently, we must pray intentionally, and we must pray fervently, believing that God will reward us in due season if we do not quit. In this chapter, I want to discuss persistence in praise.

Praise is an offering to God, and it is something that we must always be willing to give Him. Unfortunately, there are some people who will only praise God when things are going well in their lives. There are those who will suppress or withhold their praise to God because of something that someone has done to them. They shut down their praise as if God has not done anything for them. I encourage you not to be that person!

Generally speaking, praise is a **commendation** bestowed upon someone for their personal virtues or their worthy actions. In the case of God, praise is the commendation that we bestow upon Him for all He has done in our lives. Praise is not just idle adoration, but praise has substance associated with it, and each person has to make praise personal to them. I want to share three things that substantiate my praise.

First, the cause of my praise

Psalm 107 is one of the longer Psalms, and it is a general call for everyone to give God thanks through the act of praise. Everyone should praise God, no matter what may be going on in their individual lives. There is a subtle distinction between the words *praise* and *worship*. Here is the distinction: we worship God for who He is. He is God! He is the Almighty. He is the Maker of heaven and earth. He is the Ruler of the universe! He is Alpha and Omega! He is the Beginning and the End! We worship God for who He is.

However, we praise God for what He has done or is doing in our lives. Not only has God provided the basic necessities of life, like food, clothing, and shelter, He has also done so much more than that. If you are reading this book, I would like for you to pause for a moment and reflect upon the things that God has done in your life. Selah.

Everyone has at least one reason to give God praise. But if you are like most people, your praise is not rooted in only one thing that God has done in your life. Neither is it rooted in two or three things. In actuality, there are so many reasons for giving God praise that no one is able to count them all. Think about it! There are so many ways God has blessed you, so many doors that He has opened for you, so many times He has brought you peace in the midst of a storm. These are but a few reasons to give God praise.

As you know, the book of Psalms is a praise-oriented book. A look at Psalm 107 reveals some wonderful insights regarding praise. Verse 8 says, "Oh that men would praise the Lord for His goodness and for His wonderful works to the children of men."

The psalmist repeats these same words in verse 15, "Oh that men would praise the Lord for His goodness and for His wonderful works to the children of men." He repeats them once again in verse

21, "Oh that men would praise the Lord for His goodness and for His wonderful works to the children of men." He repeats for the final time in verse 31, "Oh that men would praise the Lord for His goodness and for His wonderful works to the children of men."

The psalmist repeats the exact same words four times in this Psalm. The number 4, in God's numerology, represents universality. Psalm 107:3 says that God has gathered His people out of the lands, from the east, from the west, from the north, and from the south. God has brought His people out of the lands where they were held captive, no matter where in the world those lands were located. In mentioning the four directions, east, west, north, and south, the psalmist is exclaiming the universal deliverance and restorative power of God. He is able to gather, and He will gather His seed from the ends of the earth.

At some point in our lives, many of us were captive in other lands, too, metaphorically speaking. For some, it may have been the land of drugs that held them captive, but now, they have been delivered! It may have been land of depression that held them captive, but now they can hold their head up. It may have been the land of lack that held them captive, but now they are able to take care of their family and themselves. Or it may have been the land of misery that held them captive, but now they can smile again.

If you are reading this book, and if you were ever captive in either of the lands that I mentioned or in some other land that I did not, I need you to understand that it was God who gathered you out of those lands. There is no land in which a person can become so deeply embedded that God cannot call them out. The cause of my praise is that God called me out of a terrible land that I was in. And the good news is that He is still calling out others.

"Oh that men would praise the Lord for His goodness and for His wonderful works to the children of men."

Secondly, the cost of my praise

Praise will cost us something sometimes. Every day will not be bright and shiny. Sometimes, the clouds are going to dim the skies.

It is during these dark times that we should not stop praising God; rather, we should allow our praise to shift to a different gear. And the gear that we shift to is called sacrifice. It is praising God when things around us are not good.

Hebrews 13:15 states, "By him therefore let us offer the sacrifice of praise to God continually, that is, the fruit of our lips giving thanks to his name."

True praise has nothing to do with external stimuli but everything to do with internal confidence, that is, our confidence in God. The sacrifice of praise comes from a humble heart that has been purified by fire. It rises from a spirit that has chosen to honor God in spite of the pain that life is causing at that moment (gotquestions. org). A spirit that says I choose to honor God in spite of what I'm going through right now.

> I will bless the LORD at all times: His praise shall continually be in my mouth. My soul shall make her boast in the LORD: the humble shall hear thereof, and be glad. O magnify the LORD with me, and let us exalt his name together. (Psalm 34:1–3)

The sacrifice of praise means to praise God continually (I will bless the Lord at all times). It means to praise God openly (His praise shall continually be in my mouth). It means to praise God heartily (my soul shall make her boast in the Lord).

When we don't feel like praising God, we praise Him anyway. Why do we? Because our praise to God is an offering that has nothing to do with how we happen to be feeling at that moment, but everything to do with what God is doing in that moment. And we must know in our spirits that God is moving and that He is working things out for our good (Romans 8:28). That is the cost of my praise.

Thirdly, the conclusion of my praise

Psalm 34:2 states, "My soul shall make her boast in the LORD: the humble shall hear thereof, and be glad."

Praise has a proximity blessing attached to it. So I advise you to spend time or hang around people who do not mind praising God. What David is saying is that when I offer to God the sacrifice of praise, those who know of my situation will see me praising Him. They know what I'm going through, yet they see me praising God. And the fact that I am praising God and not collapsing under the weight of my problems sends to them a strong message.

And the message is this: if God is able to hold up my brother or my sister through all that he or she is going through, then I am confident that God will enable me to stand during my test and trial as well. *The Living Bible* says, "I will boast of all his kindness to me." So David is saying that through his praise, he is actually boasting or bragging on his God. The God who is able to save. David said in verse 6, "This poor man cried out and the Lord saved him out of all his troubles."

So the conclusion of our praise should be us bragging about our God—about how great our God is! About what our God can do. About how good our God is. Christian artist Chris Tomlin gave us these wonderful words in his song "How Great Is Our God":

> The splendor of the King; Clothed in majesty.
> Let all the earth rejoice, all the earth rejoice;
> He wraps Himself in light; And darkness tries to hide,
> And trembles at His voice, trembles at His voice.
>
> How great is our God!
>
> And age to age He stands. And time is in His hands.
> Beginning and the End, Beginning and the End.
> The Godhead, Three in One. Father, Spirit, Son.
> The Lion and the Lamb, the Lion and the Lamb
>
> How great is our God!

Questions to ponder

1. How can I become more persistent in my praise?
2. What are some things that may be limiting my praise?
3. What can I do to continually make my boast in the Lord?

❀

Chapter 4

PERSISTENCE IN THANKFULNESS

*In everything give thanks: for this is the
will of God in Christ Jesus concerning you.*

—1 Thessalonians 5:18

Most theologians would agree that 1 Thessalonians 5:18 is without a doubt one of the most challenging scriptures in the Bible. The writer here is the Apostle Paul, and he says, "In everything give thanks: for this is the will of God in Christ Jesus concerning you." The structure of this verse makes it a command. Thus, we believers are commanded to give thanks to the God in everything. Notice the words here; not thanks *for* everything, but thanks *in* everything! There is a big difference in the aforementioned wording. Paul is not saying that we should necessarily thank God for our trials; rather, He is saying that we should thank God in our trials, that is, as we go through them. It is important to understand that believers are not immune from trials. Believers experience trials just like everyone else.

In our desire to honor God, often our faithfulness is challenged by unforeseen circumstances that come our way. If not handled properly, these circumstances may cause us to become stagnant in our godly pursuits. Thankfulness to God is the key to remaining persistent during challenging situations and for fighting off the spirit of stagnation.

Certainly, we should thank God for all He has given us, but beyond, this we should thank God in living, as we process in and out of life's situations. And sometimes life's situations can be overwhelming. Nevertheless, we are commanded by God to be thankful in life. Now let's be real. To be thankful for the good things that happen in our lives is relatively easy, but to be thankful in all that happens in our lives—the good and the bad, the moments of joy as well as the moments of sorrow, our successes as well as our failures, the rewards as well as the rejections—well, that requires deeper spiritual work. Nevertheless, we are commanded by God to be thankful in life.

In her book, The Gift of Thanks, Margaret Visser uses three things to convey the power of thankfulness, which is gratitude. She uses analogies of soil, lubricant, and glue.

- *Analogy of soil* refers to the heart of the person. When thankfulness is in the heart, the heart or the soil is able to be cultivated into a disposition that is pleasant. On the contrary, when thankfulness has left the heart, all that remains is a hard, dry, unkind, mean disposition. And that's not how God wants His children to be.
- *Analogy of lubricant* refers to interactions with people. When thankfulness is a part of a person's life, it oils relationships and causes understanding and peace to abide. On the other hand, when thankfulness has moved out, all that remains is coldness and indifference, and it leads to schisms and divisions. And that's not what God wants for His children.
- *Analogy of glue* refers to the unity and togetherness. This points to the oneness that thankfulness supplies. It enables us to connect with people who may still be struggling to get their lives together. But when there is no thankfulness, there is no glue. So we don't have any patience with others

who are not as spiritually mature as we are. So then we look down on those who are struggling, and we forget the expectation of God that we are to be our brother's keeper.

Thankfulness on our part enables us to be better servants for God in both spiritual and practical ways. People who are truly thankful to God know how to say thank you. There is the story of a little boy. We'll call him Johnny, who was treated to a kids' style restaurant by his grandparents.

Once they left the restaurant, little Johnny's grandparents asked him, "Are you thankful that we treated you?"

Little Johnny responded by saying, "I'm thankful, but I just don't feel like saying it."

Don't be like little Johnny; tell God thank-you in everything that you are facing. In everything, give thanks! Being thankful makes us better for God.

Some people have packaged their lives into two compartments. Compartment *A* holds all the things that they wish to forget, and compartment *B* holds all the things that they wish to remember. But here lies the problem: as long as we keep dividing our lives between good events and bad events, we cannot truly claim the fullness of our beings as the workmanship of God.

The psalmist says in Psalm 31:15, "My times are in thy hand." In other words, God guides every one of our footsteps. We must learn to look at everything that has brought us to this present moment. And then, we trust God to lead and guide us from this moment on, no matter what life throws our way in the future.

The psalmist also says in Psalm 139:13, "For thou hast possessed my reins: thou hast covered me in my mother's womb." I feel as if I am writing this directly to someone. God had you covered, even before you were born. And since you have been born, everything that you ever went through, God has used it to get you to where you are now. And for that reason, you should be thankful.

Thankfulness must be based upon something that is unchanging. Our thankfulness should never be based on that which is material. Material things are temporal in nature and are therefore subject to change. True thankfulness must be based on something that is unchanging or eternal. We are thankful for our health. We are thankful for our families and our homes. We are thankful for jobs. And we should be thankful for these. But all these things are subject to change. Your health can break down. Families can split up. Homes can be lost. Jobs can shut down. Bank accounts can dry up. If your thankfulness is based on these things, then what do you do when these things are no longer there?

Here is my plea to you! Be thankful for what you have, but do not make what you have the basis for your thankfulness. Look beyond what you have, and see what God has really given you. He has given you some things that will never change.

Thank God for being God

In the midst of *our* trials, He is still *our* God (trials don't change God). We can thank Him in the midst of our trials because we know that He has promised to be with us and that He will help us. And we know that our trials only come to make us strong (1 Peter 1:7–9).

In the midst of *our* persecutions, He is still *our* God (He knows how much we can bear). We can thank Him in the midst of our persecutions because we know that if we suffer with Him on earth, we shall reign with Him in glory (2 Timothy 2:12).

In the midst of *our* failures, He is still *our* God (God forgives). We can thank Him in the midst of our failures because we know that if we confess our sins, that He is faithful and just to forgive our sins and to cleanse us from all unrighteousness (1 John 1:9).

We can thank Him because we know that He can use our suffering and our issues to draw us closer to Himself. So thank God for being God.

Thank God for the people He has placed in your life

It is so easy to take people for granted or even to complain and become angry at them because they do not meet our every wish. But we need to give thanks for those people whom God has placed in our lives: our spouses, our children, our families, and our friends. Thank God for your pastor, your shepherd, your overseer—the one whom God has assigned to be guardian over your soul.

There is a story about a lady who was commenting on her pastor. She began by stating how good of a pastor he was. She said that he speaks well, knows the Word, is caring, and is kind. Then she inserted *but* and started talking about all the things that he did not do and all the things that he should do. Pretty soon, the list of things after the *but* outnumbered the things before the *but*. In essence, she was expressing her overall dissatisfaction with her pastor. She was unthankful for the pastor that God had given her.

This same analogy could apply to a spouse, a child, a family member, or a friend. I'm just saying, appreciate the people that God has placed in your life. Let them know that you appreciate them and that you are thankful for them.

Thank God for the gift of His Son, Jesus Christ

God has given us the greatest gift of all—His Son, Jesus, who died on the cross and rose again, so that we can know God personally and spend eternity with Him in heaven. We were separated from God because of sin, but through Christ, we have been reconciled to God the Father, and we have been grafted into His royal family. For those who have truly given their lives to Christ, no one can undo what God has done. Thank God for the permanence of your salvation. Without Christ, there would be nothing to be thankful for because everything else is like sinking sand, it just cannot stand.

Thank God for His continued presence and power in your life

God has promised that He will never leave us nor forsake us (Hebrews 13:5c).

Psalm 23:4 states, "Yea though I walk through the valley of the shadow of death, I will fear no evil, because THOU ART WITH ME." God is with us through it all.

Isaiah 43:2 states, "When thou passest through the waters, I will be with thee; and through the rivers, they shall not overflow thee: when thou walkest through the fire, thou shalt not be burned; neither shall the flame kindle upon thee."

God's presence is with us daily, and His purpose is to bring us through whatever we are facing. So it is imperative that we remain persistent in our thankfulness to Him. As I close the chapter of the book, I refer again to the Word of God through the pen of Apostle Paul in 1 Thessalonians 5:18, using various translations:

> In everything give thanks: for this is the will of God in Christ Jesus concerning you. (KJV)

> Whatever happens, keep thanking God because of Jesus Christ. This is what God wants you to do. (CEV)

> In every situation [no matter what the circumstances] be thankful and continually give thanks to God; for this is the will of God for you in Christ Jesus. (AMP)

> No matter what happens, always be thankful, for this is God's will for you who belong to Christ Jesus. (TLB)

Questions to ponder

1. How can I learn to give God thanks in all things?
2. How can I show better appreciation for the people God has placed in my life?
3. How can I learn to rest in God's presence?

Chapter 5

PERSISTENCE IN FAITH

My brethren, count it all joy when you fall into divers
temptations; knowing this, that the trying of your faith
worketh patience. But let patience have her perfect work,
that ye may be perfect and entire, wanting nothing.

—James 1:2–4

My friends, be glad, even if you have a lot of trouble.
You know that you learn to endure by having your faith tested.
But you must learn to endure everything, so that you will
be completely mature and not lacking in anything.

—James 1:2–4 (CEV)

Dear brothers, is your life full of difficulties and temptations?
Then be happy, for when the way is rough, your patience has a
chance to grow. So let it grow, and don't try to squirm out of your

problems. For when your patience is finally in full bloom, then you will be ready for anything, strong in character, full and complete.

—James 1:2–4 (TLB)

Consider it a sheer gift, friends, when tests and challenges come at you from all sides. You know that under pressure, your faith-life is forced into the open and shows its true colors. So don't try to get out of anything prematurely. Let it do its work so you become mature and well-developed, not deficient in any way.

—James 1:2–4 (MSG)

I am particularly drawn to the Message Bible translation (MSG) shown above. It shows that a believer's faith, from time to time, is placed under pressure. This pressure comes from all sides and aims to weaken or destroy the believer's faith in God. Faith is the most valuable weapon in a believer's arsenal. The scripture teaches that without faith, it is impossible to please God (Hebrews 11:6). And as it relates to daily living, the scripture teaches that the just shall live by faith (Hebrews 10:38). Hence, faithful living requires persistence in faith.

In his epistle, James was writing to the twelve tribes of Israel, who were scattered across the known world of that day. They were scattered because of severe persecution and the extreme challenges that had come their way. These were God's chosen people, yet their faith was under pressure.

In August of 2016, the area of south Louisiana where I reside faced a tremendous challenge. The challenge was an unusual weather phenomenon in which it rained steadily and heavily for three days. The amount of rain that fell caused massive flooding across four adjacent parishes in the state. Approximately seventy-five thousand structures, including houses, schools, churches, and businesses, were flooded. Within this number, some forty thousand homes were flooded. In addition to this, it is estimated that over one hundred thousand vehicles were likewise flooded. The total financial loss to the people of the state was in excess of eight billion dollars.

People who had been living comfortably in their homes only days before were no longer living in their home but were now scattered abroad. Some were living with other family members, some with friends, some in rented spaces, and some were in emergency shelters. The people were now scattered, not because of persecution, but as the result of an act of God. And I might add that many of the people whose homes sustained flooding, and perhaps the majority of them, were Christians. Without a doubt, the faith of the people impacted by this act of God was under pressure.

The historic flood of 2016 was an act of God. I say that because no one has power over rain to make it start, nor do they have power over a weather system, to make it hover over a region for several days. Only God has such a power.

As a Christian, how do you remain persistent in faith when your faith is under so much pressure? James provides us with the answer.

First, he says, "Count it all joy" (verse 2)

In verse 2, James says that believers are to "count it all joy." The Greek word for *count* is *hayg-eh'-om-ahee*, which means to have the rule over. In other words, we are to have the rule over our joy, when we encounter life's STUFF, as I call it. STUFF is *s*ituations, *t*rials, *u*ncertainties, *f*ailures, and *f*iascos. The *King James* translation refers to life's stuff as being "diver's temptations." The *Contemporary English Version* calls life's stuff "lot of trouble." *The Living Bible* calls life's stuff "difficulties and temptations." The *Message Bible* calls life's stuff "tests and challenges."

In all translations, the message is the same. And the message is that we should take authority over our joy when life issues happen. We must never allow the life's STUFF to steal our joy. A trial or a hardship is not an occasion for joy, and James is not suggesting that we act as though they are enjoyable. They are not. However, God is able to use our hardships to make us more serviceable for His kingdom.

When faith is tested, it becomes battle-hardened, which makes it stronger. Such a faith is not easily compromised. The joy part comes in when we begin to understand that the trying of our faith has purpose in it. And through God, He will cause us to endure and come out better. Consider the words of Peter:

> Wherein ye greatly rejoice, though now for a season, if need be, ye are in heaviness through manifold temptations: That the trial of your faith, being much more precious than of gold that perisheth, though it be tried with fire, might be found unto praise and honour and glory at the appearing of Jesus Christ. (1 Peter 1:6–7)

We often sing a song at our church that was recorded by gospel artist Dorothy Norwood titled "I Still Have Joy." The lyrics are as follows:

> I still have joy, I still have joy,
>> After all the things I've been through, I still
> have joy

True joy for a believer is not based on what they have acquired or what they are going through. It is based on the fact that, above all, we have Christ, and our connection with God the Father is secure through Him.

Next, James informs us that the trial is nothing but a test (verse 3)

> You know that under pressure, your faith-life is forced into the open and shows its true colors. (MSG)

I was blessed by many people who lost practically everything during the historic flood of 2016. I was blessed by the faith that they showed, even though they had lost so much. In the aftermath of the flood, I assisted in the cleaning out of three different homes, which sustained significant damage from the flood. In each case, I was blessed by the homeowner's faith. Each homeowner's faith was strong, and they all seemed to have a determination within that could only come from God. Each of them said to me something like this, "I know that God's got me in this. And, therefore, I am not worried about anything. It is tough seeing all this damage and all the things that I have lost. It is tough having to go through this, but I am not worried. Because I know that God's got me."

God uses tests to grow our faith. And faith cannot grow unless it is put under pressure. The Bible says, "Faith cometh by hearing and hearing by the word of God" (Romans 10:17). Faith indeed comes by hearing, but it grows by pressure. Job said, "Though he slay me, yet will I trust him" (Job 13:15).

The outgrowth of faith under pressure is patience. Patience is spiritual perseverance and endurance. God uses trials to develop us spiritually, in the way an athlete uses exercise to strengthen his or her muscles and to develop physical endurance. The Greek word from which the word *patience* is translated is *hoop-om-on-ay*, which means endurance or continuous waiting. I mentioned Job in chapter 1 and through all of his trials, he said these words: "All the days of my appointed time will I wait, til my change comes" (Job 14:14b). The trial is a test, and you will pass the test if you hold on to your faith.

Finally, James lets us know that God has a plan for us in the trial (verse 4)

He says, "Let patience have her perfect work, and you will be complete, you will be whole, you will be mature, you will be entire and not lacking anything." However, in order for us to get to this point in our spiritual development, we have to go through the trials at hand. I heard an old preacher say that if God brings it to you, He will bring you through it. In other words, we have been chosen by God for such a time as this. God has a plan for His children which He has articulated through many of the prophets and through the Lord Jesus Himself. However, His words through the mouth of the prophet Jeremiah speak loudly concerning His plan for His people. "'For I know the plans I have for you,' declares the LORD, 'plans to prosper you and not to harm you, plans to give you hope and a future'" (Jeremiah 29:11 NIV).

You may be in the middle of a trial right now but understand that God has a plan to bring you out of it, and when He does, you shall be better. You may be in the struggle right now but understand that God has a plan to bring you through it, and when He does, you shall be stronger. You may be in the fire right now but understand that God has a plan to bring you out of it, and when He does, you shall be like fine gold.

I encourage you to remain persistent in your faith. Persistent faith is faith that does not quit. It is faith that pushes ahead despite setbacks and challenges. It is the kind of faith that pleases God.

Questions to ponder

1. How can I become more persistent in my faith?
2. What challenges am I now facing that may impact my faith?
3. How can I better trust God in the process of my development?

Chapter 6

PERSISTENCE IN GODLY PURSUITS

Brethren, I count not myself to have apprehended: but this one thing I do, forgetting those things which are behind, and reaching forth unto those things which are before, I press toward the mark for the prize of the high calling of God in Christ Jesus. Let us therefore, as many as be perfect, be thus minded: and if in anything ye be otherwise minded, God shall reveal even this unto you.

—Philippians 3:13–15

Apostle Paul writes in verse 14, "I press toward the mark for the prize of the high calling of God in Christ Jesus." Notice that Paul uses the phrase "I press toward the mark." Though he uses the word *press*, readers often mistakenly infer the word *push*. Though both words are similar, the word press has a different connotation than push. The word push would be like that of a shove. It implies a single exertion of force. But the word press implies that the push is continual, it is constant, it is ongoing, and it is nonstop. So Paul is saying that his pursuit of the mark of the prize of the high calling of God is continual, constant, ongoing, and nonstop.

Faithful living requires pressing on or demonstrating persistence in godly pursuits, especially when the odds become stacked against us. To fully appreciate verse 14, we must put it into context within the entirety of the chapter. In this chapter, chapter 3, Paul talked about deceitful people whom he encountered along the way (verses 1–2). He talked about his religious credentials (verses 4–6) which he now renounced and relegated them to being nothing of value, as it relates to his Christian life and living (verses 7–8). He informs his readers of his current focus by identifying three key areas that influenced the way that he lives his life (verse 10).

The first area was to "know Christ and the power of His resurrection," the second area was to know "the fellowship of Christ's sufferings," and the third area was "being made conformable to Christ's death." *The Living Bible* records it this way, "Now I have given up everything else—I have found it to be the only way to really know Christ and to experience the mighty power that brought him back to life again, and to find out what it means to suffer and to die with him."

In each of these areas, Paul's focus was on some aspect of Jesus and His life. Jesus had but one agenda and that was to seek and to save them that were lost (Luke 19:10). The pursuits of a believer must focus on both maintaining the believer's witness and exhibiting that witness before others, in an effort to win souls for Christ.

The *mark* that Paul was referring to in verse 14 is the objective of verse 10, which can be summed up in two words—*knowing Christ.* Paul's position was that knowing Christ would enable these things to manifest in his life. The *prize*, as noted by Paul in verse 14, is the personal satisfaction of having obtained the mark, along with the reward to be given in heaven for having attained this goal on earth. The *high calling of God* is the divine summons extended to all believers for salvation (King James Study Bible, 1988, Liberty University). And beyond this, Paul encouraged every believer to operate in this mindset (verse 15). Believers must remain persistent in godly pursuits. These pursuits cannot be of an on-again, off-again nature. They must be continual.

Godly pursuits always run counter to worldly pursuits. Paul in his pastoral letter to his son in the ministry, Timothy, writes these words in 1 Timothy 6:11, "But thou, O man of God, flee these things; and follow after righteousness, godliness, faith, love, patience, meekness. Fight the good fight of faith, lay hold on eternal life, whereunto thou art also called, and hast professed a good profession before many witnesses."

Paul sought to encourage and strengthen Timothy by advising him to avoid or run away from the worldly things or from those who taught and preached from a worldly perspective. He references them in verses 3–5. The *Living Bible* records his words as follows:

> Some may deny these things, but they are the sound, wholesome teachings of the Lord Jesus Christ and are the foundation for a godly life. Anyone who says anything different is both proud and stupid. He is quibbling over the meaning of Christ's words and stirring up arguments ending in jealousy and anger, which only lead to name-calling, accusations, and evil suspicions. These arguers—their minds warped by sin—don't know how to tell the truth; to them the Good News is just a means of making money. Keep away from them.

Worldly things and worldly people will have a negative impact on a believer's pursuit of godly things. Paul understood what it meant to be a true follower of Christ and his desire for Timothy to be likewise. Thus, he sought to impart wisdom into his young protégé, so that he, like Paul, would be persistent in godly pursuits. The wisdom that Paul imparts to Timothy is likewise available to us today as we read his anointed and inspired words.

Paul encourages Timothy to flee the things of worldliness and follow after the things of righteousness, which are our godly pursuits. Paul breaks down the things of righteousness, our godly pursuits, into six virtues, namely *righteousness, godliness, faith, love, patience,* and *meekness.* I want to discuss each of these virtues so that I can provide clarity around what each one entails and how we, as believers, must remain persistent in pursuit of them.

First, a look at righteousness

Righteousness, in this context, is practical correctness confirming to God's will in one's thinking and acting (King James Study Bible, 1988, Liberty University). In a broader sense, it is defined as being acceptable to God. Righteousness can never be birthed by the will of man or man's efforts; it can only be God imputed unto man, by God. Without God, man will never possess righteousness.

Man is totally unable to please God in his sinful state (Romans 8:8). It is only through the grace and mercy of God can man be changed and made acceptable to God. When we pursue the character of Christ, we pursue righteousness. A proper understanding that righteousness comes only through and from God will prevent one from developing a spirit of self-righteousness, which is contrary to the will of God. The starting point for pursuing righteousness is a humble heart. See the following scriptures:

> Humble thyself in the sight of the Lord, and He shall lift you up. (James 4:10)

> Humble yourselves therefore under the mighty hand of God, that He may exalt you in due time. (1 Peter 5:6)

A humble heart is one that seeks the presence of God continually. I recently saw an article posted on the Internet on May 6, 2018, by Gina. The article was titled "5 Everyday Ways to Pursue God's Righteousness." I like to share the following excerpts from the posting with a few extensions of my own:

1. Seek God's presence. Spend quality time with God.
2. Walk in the Spirit. Follow the Holy Spirit's guidance daily.

3. Invite wisdom. Ask God for wisdom in decision-making.
4. Be generous. Be a blessing to others. Generosity is a by-product of our pursuit of righteousness.
5. Don't be shortsighted. Understand that God's plan is beyond what you and I can see.

Next, a look at godliness

Godliness is a way of life that is shaped by and based upon the principles found in the Word of God. The entire Bible is a book of godliness, and as we incorporate its teachings into our lives, we become more like it, and its teachings are then reflected in our behavior. Consider Paul's words to another protégé of his, Titus, "For the grace of God that bringeth salvation hath appeared to all men, Teaching us that, denying ungodliness and worldly lusts, we should live soberly, righteously, and godly, in this present world" (Titus 2:11–12).

In life, we will face challenges brought on by the world's system. Our response to those challenges should be godly in nature, that is, our response should demonstrate our commitment to honor God and His word.

I have been a member of the church that I now pastor for all my saved life. The pastor who baptized me was named Rev. George R. Clark, and he was truly a man of God. I am reminded of the time Pastor Clark brought to the congregation a vision to purchase land and construct a new facility. When he shared this vision to the congregation, it was accepted wholeheartedly. The pastor's vision for constructing the new facility had but one caveat, and it was that we purchase the land and build the facility without borrowing any money. In other words, we were to do the project debt-free.

Given the fact that our congregation was not large and that we were not blessed with people of great financial worth, we knew that this would be a significant challenge for us. Nevertheless, we all were very excited. Small groups within the church began meeting to discuss ways and ideas for raising money for this project. As I recall, the choir held musicals, with the offering proceeds being dedicated to the capital campaign. Pastor Clark never liked the idea of selling dinners as a way of raising money, which was a common practice during those days, but as I recall, some dinners were sold.

The men's ministry, of which I was a part, met and came up with an idea for raising money that we all felt would be a great success. The idea that we came up with was to hold a raffle. Each man would be responsible for selling a certain number of raffle tickets for a chance to win some item of value. We assayed that if each man within our group did their part, we would net several thousand dollars from the raffle. Holding raffles was then, and still is, quite common, and it is a highly effective way for organizations to generate funds.

But there was a question of its use when it came to churches. Though many churches in and around our area used this process to raise money, the question remained, "Is raffling by a church a godly way of generating funds?" So the men decided to discuss the idea with Pastor Clark before going forth. When we met with Pastor Clark, I was amazed how he calmly and lovingly taught us a lesson on godliness, as a body of Christ. He said that certainly, the idea would likely raise lots of money, and it would get us closer to our financial target. But all that we will gain through the raffling process, he said, we will lose in our witness and a church who trusts God. He said, by holding a raffle, we would be embracing the patterns of the world while abandoning the principles of the Word, which is to freely give.

When Pastor Clark said those words, we all felt convicted in our hearts, but were thankful that we had a leader who tried to exemplify godliness and one who taught us the ways of godliness. Without the raffle, it would take us longer to generate enough funds to do the project debt-free, and it did. But we stayed the course as a congregation, and a few years later, we moved into our new, spacious facility, totally debt-free. Godliness pays great off in more ways than one. Not only did we accomplish the debt-free goal that he laid out in his vision for the project, but we now had a testimony that we could share.

On an individual note, Peter gives us these encouraging words in 2 Peter 1:3, "According as his divine power hath given unto us all things that pertain unto life and godliness, through the knowledge of him that hath called us to glory and virtue."

We have all that we need to live godly. Despite the many challenges and obstacles that may arise in our daily lives, godliness shows our devotion to God and His word through action.

A look at faith

I will not say much about faith in this segment, given that I have already discussed it in chapter 5. I will say that faith must be a godly pursuit in that faith is essential in all that we do. It is the thing that binds and undergirds the other godly pursuits. Without faith, it is impossible to please God (Hebrews 11:6). Pursue faith at all costs.

Now a look at love

Love, in the context used here, is a maturing affection for God and man. An affection that moves one to help. Christ, who is the embodiment of love, always stood on the side of the oppressed. Luke 4:18–19 (TLB) states:

> The Spirit of the Lord is upon me; he has appointed me to preach Good News to the poor; he has sent me to heal the brokenhearted and to announce that captives shall be released and the blind shall see, that the downtrodden shall be freed from their oppressors, and that God is ready to give blessings to all who come to him.

In our pursuit of the virtue of love, we must be like Christ, standing on the side of the oppressed or those who have been relegated to a lesser status or those who have become marginalized by society. In her podcast on Crosswalk.com, Debbie Holloway posted an article titled "5 Ways the Bible Shows us How to Live with Love." I'd like to share those five ways with a few extensions of my own:

1. Lift up the broken, enlarge the small, and favor the weak
2. Have patience with each other. Be long-suffering, understanding, and kind.
3. Be generous. Be willing to provide aid and assistance as needed.
4. Don't withhold forgiveness. Release forgiveness willingly and quickly.
5. Keep your promises. Let you word be true.

A look at patience

Patience is defined as perseverance or steadfastness in life and service. Patience is a virtue that must be developed over time. Hence, it requires a continual effort. Often when facing life's challenges, God simply wants us to wait on Him. Wait does not mean to sit idly by; it means to continue serving, to continue doing God's will as we endure through the challenge before us.

There are many biblical figures who demonstrated patience in their struggles. Perhaps the greatest example of patience is seen in Job. I summarized Job's plight in chapter 1, so I will not go into detail here. Yet James, in his teaching on patience, held Job up as an example for us to follow (James 5:11).

Another person who demonstrated patience was Abraham. Abraham (Abram) received a promise from God that he would bear a child through his wife Sarah (Sarai). The only problem was that at the time when Abram was given the promise, he was seventy-five years old, and his wife Sarai was sixty-six, and she was barren or could not have children. Yet Abram believed God, and at the age of ninety-nine years old, his wife, now called Sarah, gave birth to their child named Isaac. "And so, after he had patiently endured, he obtained the promise" (Hebrews 6:15).

Patience is a virtue that is much needed in society and is a godly pursuit that believers should always keep at the forefront.

Finally, a look at meekness

Some people wrongly view meekness as cowardice or spineless-ness. However, meekness is a virtue and a strength. *Meekness* is the quality of a heart that has been humbled by God. Believers must pursue meekness at all costs by allowing God to be God and recognizing that without Him, we are nothing.

Jesus, who is God in the flesh, identified Himself as being meek. "Come unto me, all ye that labour and are heavy laden, and I will give you rest. Take my yoke upon you, and learn of me; for I am meek and lowly in heart: and ye shall find rest unto your souls."

Becoming meek, too, is an ongoing process. Meekness requires relinquishing a selfish ideal for the greater good of Christ and ministry. There is a promise from Christ to those who are meek. He said in Matthew 5:5, "*Blessed are the meek for they shall inherit the earth.*"

Probably the best example of meekness is found in John the Baptist who had significantly gained notoriety through the baptizing of many people. John the Baptist even baptized Jesus himself (Matthew 3:13–17). After being baptized by John, Jesus stayed in Judea for a while, and he began baptizing people there. John, on the other hand, traveled to Aenon, near Salim, and he began baptizing people there.

This narrative is found in John 3:22–30, and it records that there arose an argument between a person and John the Baptist's followers. This person was arguing that Jesus's baptism was best or better than John's baptism. So John the Baptist's followers decided to bring the issue to John. See the following from *The Living Bible*, "So they came to John and said, 'Master, the man you met on the other side of the Jordan River—the one you said was the Messiah—he is baptizing too, and everybody is going over there instead of coming here to us.'"

John's followers were obviously concerned that Jesus was now attracting all the people to Himself. Note John's response:

John replied, "God in heaven appoints each man's work. My work is to prepare the way for

Donald R. Ruth

that man so that everyone will go to him. You yourselves know how plainly I told you that I am not the Messiah. I am here to prepare the way for him—that is all. The crowds will naturally go to the main attraction—the bride will go where the bridegroom is! A bridegroom's friends rejoice with him. I am the Bridegroom's friend, and I am filled with joy at his success. He must become greater and greater, and I must become less and less."

John the Baptist understood his role and his mission. He never developed the *big head* about who he was. He willingly relinquished his ideals for the greater work of God, and he taught those who followed him the same. This is what meekness is all about.

Faithful living involves persistence in godly pursuits. God's work and His glory must be our sole aim, and we will accomplish much, if we remain persistent.

Questions to ponder

1. How can I become more persistent in my godly pursuits overall?
2. In which area do I find myself struggling the most?
3. What can I do, specifically, to build my strength in this area?

Conclusion

I trust that this book has been a blessing to you, and it is my prayer that you will resolve, never to quit, or give up. Certainly, life has its share of struggles, and as I said earlier, the fact that we are believers does not immune us from life's struggles. However, despite the struggles we often face, the expectation of God is clear; we are stewards of the mysteries of God, and it is required in stewards to be found faithful.

As a reminder, living a faithful life simply means remaining committed to God in all things, despite challenges and obstacles. Faithfulness boils down to persistency, that is, staying the course laid out by God. God will always reward faithfulness, and remember that there is a blessing and benefit to being faithful.

Hebrews 3:14 (NLT) states, "For if we are faithful to the end, trusting God just as firmly as when we first believed, we will share in all that belongs to Christ."

God bless you as you live faithfully before God!